A CULTURE OF PRAYER

FUELING REVIVAL AND TRANSFORMATION

BOOK TWO

COREY JONES & ROB MCCORKLE

Published by Fire School Ministries
FireSchoolMinistries.com

ISBN: 978-1-953285-72-0

Fire School Ministries
P.O. Box 667
Pickerington, OH 43147

Or email:
fireschoolministries@gmail.com

Many of the Greek definitions are taken from Rick Renner, *Sparkling Gems from the Greek* (Tulsa, OK: Teach All Nations, 2003), Rick Meyer, e-Sword, www.e-sword.net/downloads.html, and Logos Bible Software 5.

NOTE: Portions of some Scripture quotations have been bolded, italicized and/or underlined for didactic emphasis.

Cover design by Nate Braxton — nbraxton@gmail.com
Interior design by D.E. West — www.emoondesigns.com w/ Dust Jacket Press
Compilation by Rob McCorkle
Edited by Cathy Burgess and Cindy McCorkle

Printed in the United States of America

CONTENTS

INTRODUCTION

There's a particular chapter in the book of Acts that often refocuses my attention to the need for prayer. The early church was approximately six years old and grown to over 10,000 believers in Jerusalem. However, because of some organizational problems the apostles called a "board meeting" of sorts with all the disciples. They identified the problem, agreed upon a solution, and appointed fellow disciples to carry out the solution while holding fast to their calling. In Acts 6:4, they stated, "But we will devote ourselves to prayer and the ministry of the word."

Devoting ourselves to prayer must be our priority, otherwise it will be replaced with the demands of the urgent. Every pastor, church, and believer can identify with how quickly the immediate overshadows the ultimate. The enemy is all too happy when we abandon the place of prayer for the demands of life. What's true for the individual is true for the Church, too. Many churches forsake the "Minister" for ministry and spend time talking *about* Jesus rather than *to* Him.

I remember hearing Leornard Ravenhill say, "Prayer often becomes like a starting pistol before a main event when prayer *is* the main event." I believe that is what the apostles were stating to the newly birthed church in Acts. The main event at the genesis of the early congregation was prayer (Acts 1:14), but the leadership six years later had to make it abundantly clear that prayer was still a main priority. Our prayer for you as you read this book is that the main event of your life and ministry will be prayer.

Since the release of the first book in this series, Corey and I have continued to hear stories of believers prioritizing their lives around prayer. Even more, we have learned of churches that have made prayer the central activity that fuels their mission.

Recently, we held a conference for a church that transformed their choir rehearsal room into a prayer room. They still sing and worship, but they are devoting themselves to the one activity that fans the flames to their praise of God. Beyond that, they are experiencing many more spiritual transformations because prayer has become the main event.

I stated in the first book of this series that these books are short, simple, and straight to the point. They are not intended to be an exhaustive discourse about prayer, but a primer to enhance your prayer life. To put it bluntly, we would rather you pray than merely read about it. Our suggestion is to read one chapter each day for a week. Small groups and prayer teams have used the first book to help focus their attention on prayer. These are merely options, we urge you to pray and ask God to direct you to use this book to develop a lifestyle of prayer.

Most assuredly, these books are for all disciples of Christ who long to be close to Him and hear His voice. Prayer is as much listening as speaking, and its purpose is far beyond obtaining answers. Prayer is how we slow down to catch Jesus. It's how we yield our heart to Him and discover our identity, value, and purpose. Prayer unites the ordinary with the extraordinary and results in our colaboring with Him to manifest the kingdom of God on earth.

So, open your heart to Jesus and may His presence leap off these pages. Corey and I are honored to have a small part in helping to inspire the body of Christ to remain on its knees.

In His service,
Rob McCorkle
May 2025

CHAPTER ONE

TRANSFORMING YOUTH THROUGH PRAYER

Corey Jones

What I'm witnessing at my church since 2019, especially with the youth and young adults, is nothing short of remarkable. It's not an overstatement to say that our kids are unrecognizable. The parents of our students will tell you that their kids are no longer the same.

We have been a praying church for over 20 years and have witnessed many amazing life changes, but after 2019 there was a significant shift when we established a prayer room and began praying and worshipping every day of the week—morning, noon, and night. When we established the prayer room, I believed it would impact our church in powerful and profound ways, but I never anticipated what would happen to our youth.

To my surprise, our youth and young adults quickly got involved in the prayer room, some even began teaching themselves how to play instruments so they could lead worship. I think we were all a bit shocked by what we were witnessing, especially the parents. Every Thursday and Friday night, many of the youth and young adults fill the prayer room, devoting hours to worship, prayer, and meditation on the Word.

The transformation in the lives of our students has been dramatic. Kids who once battled anxiety, depression, and even suicidal ideation have experienced total freedom and deliverance. The level of spiritual hunger and maturity has been incredible to witness.

Simply, we are witnessing a corporate outpouring of the Holy Spirit on the younger generation through prayer and worship. Just like everyone in the upper room was filled with the Holy Spirit on the Day of Pentecost in Acts 2, the impact of the Holy Spirit's activity in the lives of our students has been transformative.

Remember Jesus promised His disciples that the Holy Spirit would be given in response to their prayers (Luke 11:13), and Paul made the connection between the infilling of the Holy Spirit and corporate worship: "Do not get drunk on wine, which leads to debauchery. Instead, be filled with the Spirit, speaking to one another with psalms, hymns, and songs from the Spirit. Sing and make music from your heart to the Lord, always giving thanks to God the Father for everything, in the name of our Lord Jesus Christ" (Ephesians 5:18-20).

Paul spoke of the infilling of the Holy Spirit taking place in the context of worship that flows from the heart. When people dedicate themselves to worship and prayer, the Spirit is drawn, and people are filled. Instead of witnessing another generation of young people being destroyed by addictions to drugs, alcohol, and pornography, we are witnessing a generation of youth turning to Jesus and being filled with the Spirit.

In truth, I believe that the best way to describe what is happening to our youth is that the Holy Spirit is making Jesus real to them. Jesus is not a religion of rules, but a real person to our children and youth. They've locked eyes with Him at an early age, and now they are driven by one desire and that is to gaze on the beauty of the Lord, like David described in Psalm 27. In fact, Jesus is more real to them than the world around them and as a result, many of our students are sensing calls to ministry in the church.

I think it's incredibly insightful and revelatory that after Jesus cleansed the temple and declared that His Father's house would be a house of prayer, the first people to respond in worship and faith were children: "But when the chief priests and the teachers of the law saw the wonderful things [Jesus] he did and the children shouting in the temple courts, 'Hosanna to the Son of David,' they were indignant. 'Do you hear what these children are saying?' they asked him. 'Yes,' replied Jesus, 'have you never read, "'From the lips of children and infants you, Lord, have called forth your praise'" (Matthew 21:15-16)?

Think about it: Kids love to shout, sing, pray, and praise. So, when a church has a prayer culture, the younger generation will respond in worship. We may have stumbled upon the secret of not losing students when they leave the youth ministry. Sadly, statistics indicate that over 85% of young people who are raised in the church leave the faith after they graduate from high school.

The reason why such a staggering number of kids fall away is because they don't really know the exalted Jesus whose eyes are like fire. What's missing is many churches don't have a culture of prayer and until every church is a house of prayer, we will continue to see many youth and young adults drift into the world and become prodigals rather than passionate followers of Jesus.

My constant prayer for the children and youth of our generation is that they would be captured by the same driving passion that led young David to pray these words: "One thing I ask from the Lord, this only do I seek: that I may dwell in the house of the Lord all the days of my life, to gaze on the beauty of the Lord and to seek him in his temple" (Psalms 27:4).

PRAYER POINTS

- Take some time to pray for children and youth. Pray that their hearts are set afire to pray.
- Ask the Lord to give you insight on how to reach young people through prayer, prayer groups, and worship events.
- Pray about what it would look like to pray morning, noon, and night. Ask Him how this might impact your family, your church, and the youth.

CHAPTER TWO

SPIRIT-LED PRAYER

Rob McCorkle

Often when I teach, I state that believers must replicate Jesus. That statement is the essence of holiness and our credal belief as a Church. Let it sink in for a moment. All of us, through the redemptive work of Christ, have the capacity to be just like Jesus.

In John 14:12, Jesus said, "Truly, truly, I say to you, he who believes in Me, the works I do, he will do also; and greater works than these he will do; because I go to the Father." That statement is almost too incredible to believe, which is why Jesus started by saying, "truly, truly". In that culture, to begin a sentence in that manner meant what you were being told was absolute truth and you needed to believe it.

But doing what Jesus did and even greater works is dependent upon Jesus going to the Father so that the Holy Spirit could be distributed. Jesus said elsewhere that it was to our advantage that He leave so that He could send the Helper, the Holy Spirit to us (John 16:7). Our ability to replicate Jesus is not possible unless we are sourced with the same Holy Spirit that operated through Him. Yet when you and I are empowered and led by the Spirit, we most certainly can accomplish the works of Jesus and even greater if needed.

That's what makes the next verse so interesting, Jesus immediately talked about prayer. "Whatever you ask in My name, that will I do, so that the Father may be glorified in the Son" (John 14:13). I propose that doing the works of Jesus is specifically tied to prayer. In other words, if I'm not praying, I will never be able to live like Jesus. Prayer, then, becomes the avenue that transforms my life so that I'm truly Christlike.

The aspect that really challenges me is that Jesus said, "Whatever you ask in My name, that I will do". Frankly, that means anything is possible. However, through the years, the "whatever you ask" has been used in all sorts of ways. When we pastored, Cindy and I would have people approach us with a long list of requests, and they would quote this passage of Scripture. "Whatever" they would say, "Jesus said whatever we asked in His name." Some things that people were petitioning God for seemed legitimate, wholesome, and even beneficial to the kingdom of God.

But let's be honest, I have no clue *whatever* to ask. I might think I know what's best or what I should pray in each situation, but if truth be told, I need help. That is exactly why Jesus continued, "I will ask the Father, and

He will give you another Helper, that He may be with you forever" (John 14:16). The gift of the Holy Spirit that Jesus talked about in this context can lead me to pray in a manner that enables me to fulfill His works.

Truly, the Helper—Holy Spirit—is the One who helps me with every aspect of my life, especially with knowing what to pray and how to pray. When the disciples requested of Jesus to teach them to pray (Luke 11:2), I believe they understood the single activity that empowered His life and ministry. They didn't ask for lessons on multiplying bread, how to walk on water, or even how to raise the dead. They sought to be schooled in prayer.

All of us need to be schooled in the essential activity of prayer. There is too much at stake these days not to be like Jesus and do what He did. We don't need religion. We don't need more pious sentiments or rants posted on Facebook. We don't need bigger churches or better programs. We need people who replicate Jesus in every facet of their life.

We need Christ followers who are being perpetually sourced by the Holy Spirit doing the works of Jesus. And when it comes to prayer, we need believers who can bring heaven to earth because they are praying Spirit-led prayers.

Ask the Holy Spirit to give you the "whatever" to pray for. Instead of approaching God with a list, pause in His presence and let Him give you the agenda for prayer. When I led our corporate prayer time during our pastorate, we would linger and wait for the leadership of His presence. It wasn't long until the Holy Spirit would guide our prayer meeting into a specific direction. Sometimes the results to our prayers were immediate with miracles of healing or spiritual transformation in the service. But when the Spirit led our prayers, we were certain the impossible was plausible and the works of Jesus were going to manifest.

PRAYER POINTS

- Ask the Holy Spirit to teach you to pray like Jesus.
- Linger in His presence and ask Him what you should pray.
- Yield your heart and life to the sourcing of the Holy Spirit. Ask Him to empower you so you can be just like Jesus.

CHAPTER THREE

THE AWE OF PRAYER

Corey Jones

Every Wednesday night at our prayer meeting we gather early with the staff and leaders to listen and pray with the help of the Holy Spirit. Learning to listen and hear God's heart is critical to a powerful prayer meeting. We never want to pray what's on our minds, but rather we seek to pray what's in the Father's heart. We want to clearly hear what the Spirit is saying to our church, so we spend much of the day fasting, waiting, and listening.

We don't emphasize this point enough when talking about prayer, but the key to sustaining a culture of prayer is listening rather than talking. Listening requires waiting and being still as a dedicated value and determined practice. We must cultivate a life of listening and hearing God's voice, which begins in personal prayer and meditation on the Word. As we learn to listen and hear the Father's voice in secret, we're better equipped to hear His voice in corporate gatherings of prayer.

What we are ultimately listening for is God's presence. Of course, we desire to hear words of wisdom and revelation from the Lord, but the real goal of prayer is encountering Jesus. It's in this posture of listening that we begin to ask, seek, and knock for the presence of the Holy Spirit to come and reveal Jesus to us (Luke 11:5-13). And Jesus promised that where two or three are gathered in His name in the context of agreement prayer, He would manifest and be present in our midst (Matthew 18:18-20).

During a recent prayer meeting, there was a song quietly playing in the background. It was entitled, *Yeshua.* As we all began to sing and whisper Jesus' name over and over again, suddenly the atmosphere dramatically changed. The weighty presence of Jesus was immediately realized and tangibly felt in our midst. I felt so overwhelmed by the presence of the Holy Spirit; I started weeping. My tears were really a mixture of joy and a deep sense of awe, aware of the nearness of Jesus' presence.

At one point, I found myself unable to stand, so I knelt, realizing that everyone else was on their knees or faces in the presence of the Lord. On the island of Patmos, when John heard a voice behind him, he turned around and saw that the voice speaking to him was the exalted Jesus. Immediately, he fell on his face in reverential fear (Revelation 1:17). This sense of awe and reverence is the fruit of prayer, and I don't ever want to do life or ministry without it.

In the Book of Acts, the Church was described as praying constantly together (Acts 1:14). The fruit of their constant prayers was a sudden Heavenly outpouring of the wind and fire of the Holy Spirit. At our church we often say that the key to the "suddenly" of the Spirit's coming is the "constantly" of corporate prayer.

Because of the activity of the Spirit's presence in response to the early church's devotion to prayer, there was an overwhelming sense of awe that was felt by believers and unbelievers. In fact, one of the identifiable marks of the early church was that everyone was filled with awe by the signs and wonders of the Spirit (Acts 2:43).

The fruit of this awe or reverence was that lost people were radically convicted and converted. This sense of awe is still desperately needed in the Church today. It is this awe of God's presence that brings conviction and repentance to the heart of the unbeliever.

Paul described the power and reality of this awe of God's presence resulting in unbelievers experiencing conviction and repentance. "But if an unbeliever or an inquirer comes in while everyone is prophesying, they are convicted of sin and are brought under judgment by all, as the secrets of their hearts are laid bare. So they will fall down and worship God, exclaiming, 'God is really among you'" (1 Corinthians 14:24-25).

After we began praying as a church, I witnessed the reality of the power of the Holy Spirit bringing a deep sense of awe amid our gatherings, especially among lost people, resulting in countless unbelievers experiencing conviction and turning to the Lord. One day, a precious lady who had been attending our church for several weeks called the office and asked to speak with me. Her name is Julie Moore, and she was addicted to methamphetamines and her husband had a meth lab in their home.

When I spoke with Julie on the phone, she began to cry. She asked me to explain what she kept feeling every time she came to our church. I knew what she was talking about. Julie was experiencing the tangible presence of Jesus. For the next few minutes, I shared the gospel with her and led her to the Lord. A few weeks later Julie testified that the Lord not only saved her on that phone call, but she was delivered from her addiction to meth as well. Not long after that, her husband Ron came to Christ, and the meth lab in their home was shut down.

Nothing matters more than Jesus' presence in our churches. We must learn to wait and listen for His presence. We desperately need the of awe of God to be experienced as a sign and wonder to our lost world. We desperately need to devote ourselves to being houses of prayer again.

PRAYER POINTS

- Ask the Lord what's on His mind, and spend some time listening. Ask Him to reveal how He wants you to pray about what is on His mind.
- Ask the Holy Spirit to reveal Jesus to you.
- Spend some time asking for His presence to fill the space you're in. Ask Him to fill you to overflowing.

CHAPTER FOUR

WEAKNESS AND INTERCESSION

Rob McCorkle

There is little doubt that life can throw us a curve ball now and then leaving us in a bewildered state. Perhaps you suddenly lose your job or your unmarried daughter informs you that she's pregnant. Maybe it's a diagnosis you didn't see coming or an untimely death in the family. Some people in these circumstances discover the supernatural ability to give praise to God thus fulfilling Paul's exhortation to give thanks in all situations (1 Thessalonians 5:18). Yet, there are others who find themselves at a loss for words not knowing how to pray.

Recently, Corey and I had a friend suddenly pass away. At the funeral, the echoed response was, "We don't even know what to say or pray." They are not alone. The apostle Paul said, "In the same way the Spirit also helps our weakness; for we do not know how to pray as we should…" (Romans 8:26). Sometimes we don't know how to pray as we should because of our own weakness.

Weakness (*astheneia*) has a variety of meanings, but in the context this word means an overwhelming sense of inadequacy. This word is not to be confused with fear or insecurity, although those emotions can make one feel weak and vulnerable. Weakness is an understanding or awareness of our own finiteness to make a difference in our immediate circumstances.

Paul learned this lesson when he was confronted with demonic opposition that wouldn't depart from him, even after praying three times for it to be removed. It was a messenger of Satan sent to torment (to beat and violently mistreat) Paul and he realized he was too weak to make this evil presence flee (2 Corinthians 12:7-9). Yet, Paul learned that God's grace and power were more than enough against such a foe.

In this particular situation, Paul's weakness became a portal for God's greatness. It led Paul to delight in his weaknesses so God's supernatural intervention could manifest. The same idea is expressed in Romans. Because of weakness, Paul states a person can be at a loss to know how to pray, but he continued, "...the Spirit intercedes for us with groanings too deep for words" (Romans 8:26). The Holy Spirit, the Helper as we read about in Chapter Two, helps our weakness.

Over the years, I've heard people say they had the gift of intercession; meaning, they felt called by God to pray on behalf of other people. But this is the only place in the New Testament this specific word for intercession appears, and we discover it is the Holy Spirit coming to our rescue and praying through us. He helps us, which means He grasps the situation we're burdened with and petitions through us with groanings beyond words. In addition, the Holy Spirit intercedes for us in accordance to the will of God (Romans 8:27).

Consequently, God causes all things to work together for the good of those who love Him (Romans 8:28). This truth should comfort us all when we're made aware of our weakness and don't know how to pray as we should. Weakness in God's economy can invite the power of God to manifest through us. Weakness can remind us that we really have nothing to give anyone unless the Lord supplies us with what we need (Luke 11:6). Weakness can be linked to those who are poor in spirit, and Jesus said theirs is the kingdom of heaven (Matthew 5:3).

Countless times Cindy and I have knelt before the Lord and yielded our weaknesses to Him. Like you, we have navigated through challenging family issues, sickness, tragedies, and critical decisions. We've experienced our share of demonic opposition in ministries and churches. With a loss of words and a deep sense of our own finiteness, we have found ourselves uttering to the Lord our need for His Spirit to help our weaknesses.

What about you? Maybe you're a single mom, a young married couple, a pastor or leader; maybe you're being tormented by evil. Let your weakness become an invitation for His grace to explode on your behalf. Thank God for the presence and power of the Holy Spirit who will communicate through you so that the goodness and will of God can manifest on your behalf.

PRAYER POINTS

- Take a moment to thank God for the Holy Spirit who helps in moments of weakness.
- Offer yourself to the Lord in prayer and ask Him to intercede through you, especially if you feel weak and unsure how to pray about a specific situation.
- Pray for His grace and power to manifest through you.

CHAPTER FIVE

PRAYING AND PERSEVERING LOVE

Corey Jones

A prayer that I have prayed constantly for nearly three decades and one that I believe has helped sustain my life, relationships, and ministry is a prayer that Paul prayed for the Thessalonians: "May the Lord direct your hearts into God's love and Christ's perseverance" (2 Thessalonians 3:5). It is such a simple but stabilizing prayer. Almost daily I find myself praying some form of this prayer: "Father direct my heart into your love and into the perseverance of Jesus."

Honestly, I don't think I have fully grasped what this prayer and the truth behind it has meant to me over the years, but I believe it is a prayer that my Father has answered repeatedly in my life. This powerful prayer is for anyone, but I have found it very helpful and healing as a pastor. Pastors, I believe, find it easier to preach about the love of God than to fully receive the Father's love for themselves.

Sadly, hurt and rejection come with the job description in pastoral ministry. We know it did with Jesus. Loving people is part of pastoring God's children, but I confess that at times I've had to resist bitterness, hurt, and anger toward the very people I was called to love and serve. With that said, I really believe that my daily attempts to pray this prayer have served to bring real healing to the interior parts of my soul. The Father pours His very love into my heart by the Holy Spirit as I pray.

When I pray for the Lord to direct my heart into the Father's love, I believe that what I am asking is for the Father's kindness, mercy, and forgiveness to flow into me and through me. The reality is that it's not my love that sustains me, it's the Father's love. Sadly, I believe that what has derailed many pastors, and their ministries, is the Father's love got blocked by resentment and unaddressed anger. Consequently, God's love quit freely flowing into their hearts.

In 1 Peter, we have this admonition to be spiritually alert and awake in prayer so we can keep loving: "Since we are approaching the end of all things, be intentional, purposeful, and self-controlled so that you can be given to prayer. Above all, constantly [*have*] echo God's intense love for one another, for love will be a canopy over a multitude of sins" (1 Peter 4:7-8 The Passion Translation).

The Greek note in The Passion Translation says: "The verb have (*echo*) means to maintain, possess, keep; to be so closely joined to something that you become its echo. In this case, we join ourselves so closely to God's love that we echo His forgiving, fervent love toward other people."

Truly, it is our alertness and watchfulness in prayer that sustains His love in us, because when we pray we are accessing the infinite and unending supply of God's love. The reason we must keep praying is because prayer keeps us tethered to the Father's love, enabling us to echo that love wherever we are. For anyone battling unresolved hurt and anger, I pray today that your heart would be directed into the Father's infinite supplies of love.

The second part of the prayer is equally potent and powerful in its effect. Paul prays for Christ's perseverance to fill our hearts. I think I've prayed this prayer thousands of times. I've asked for the Lord to give me Christ's perseverance, and I believe I've witnessed thousands of instances when I felt Jesus strengthen and sustain me. He's enabled me to keep going, keep standing, and keep enduring no matter how badly I wanted to give up or give in.

Satan and his demons work overtime to get all of us, especially pastors, to quit. The enemy knows that if he strikes the shepherd, the sheep will scatter. I can't tell you how many times I've heard that taunting voice trying to convince me to believe lies about myself, about people, or even about God, telling me that my time here at Crossroads Tabernacle is over and that I've done all I can do, now I need to move on. But I can't even begin to share how many times in prayer that I reached down and found Jesus' perseverance deep inside of me, steadying and sustaining me, and sending me back into the battle with renewed strength to face whatever it was I needed to face.

The truth is that Jesus didn't quit, He endured the cross and overcame, and we don't have a quitter inside of us. We are called to persevere, to keep standing, to never quit, and with Christ's perseverance within us, we will endure to the end.

In my office, I've had this sign posted above my door for about 15 years. It says: "I can't quit. I won't quit. Neither will you." For anyone feeling the taunts of the devil to throw in the towel, I pray that your heart would be directed into Jesus' perseverance, and that you would be given renewed strength to get up and throw the towel back at the adversary and accuser and keep going.

PRAYER POINTS

- Ask the Lord to fill your heart with God's love.
- Pray for the Holy Spirit to cleanse your heart from any hurt, anger, or rejection. Ask Him if there is anything that might hinder His love from flowing into and from you.
- Pray that you will persevere in the strength of the Lord. Ask God to give you the power to never quit or give up doing what He's ask you to do.

CHAPTER SIX
WATCHING AND PRAYING

Rob McCorkle

Get me talking about the Christian faith and it won't be long until I start talking about being sourced by the Holy Spirit. I can't begin to tell you the importance of our relationship to the Holy Spirit. He is a person, He desires to fill us to overflowing, and to lead us step by step into all truth. You and I need the activity of the Holy Spirit in our lives, or we'll fail in our prayers, not to mention failing in our Christian walk. Sons and daughters of God are defined as being constantly led by the Spirit (Romans 8:14).

Let's discuss how the Holy Spirit enables us to overcome demonic resistance. You don't have to walk with Christ very long to realize there is a real enemy to our faith. He operates with one goal. He comes to steal, kill, and destroy (John 10:10). Look around and you will find the carnage in marriages, families, churches, and ministries resulting from demonic assaults. However, we've been equipped to prevail against the rulers, powers, and darkness in the spirit realm.

In Ephesians 6, Paul outlines for us different pieces of armor that a Roman soldier would wear when entering a conflict so they could overcome their enemy. Each piece is essential to our spiritual protection so that when we are face to face with evil, we will stand victorious in the power of God. But let's highlight Ephesians 6:18, "With all prayer and petition pray [*praying*] at all times in the Spirit, and with this view, be on the alert [*watching*] with all perseverance and petition for all the saints" (emphasis mine).

The key to that verse is the phrase, in the Spirit (*pneumati*). This Greek word means by the Spirit, with the Spirit, or sourced (empowered) in the Spirit. It tells us that whatever is accomplished can only be done by the action and strength of the Spirit working through us. There are two present-tense verbs identified in verse 18: watching and praying, and both activities are essential when standing against demonic powers.

First, the phrase "be on the alert" stems from the word watching. It means to be alert, awake, aware, vigilant, and discerning. If there has ever been a time in history for the need of discernment, that time is now. The Bible says, "But the Spirit explicitly says that in later times some will fall away from the faith, paying attention to deceitful spirits and doctrines of demons" (1 Timothy 4:1).

When Cindy and I pastored, we taught our congregation the simple lessons of John 10. There is a Shepherd, there are sheep, and there is a thief. We're to know the shepherd, hear His voice, and be led by Him. Yet, if we're not watching, discerning, and spiritually alert, the crafty nature of the enemy will quickly mislead us.

We're to resist the enemy, yet if we're not being sourced by the Spirit, we'll become dull and undiscerning of his methods. Consider the many believers who watch, read, or look at unwise things or give their attention to things that can be misleading. These days, too many believers are stuffing their minds with social media more than the Scriptures. Paul tells us that if we're ignorant of the devil's schemes, he will take advantage of us (2 Corinthians 2:11). The Church needs to be found watching under the leadership of the Holy Spirit. God give us spiritual watchmen on the walls.

Second, Paul said, "With all prayer and petition *pray*". The word pray is a present tense verb and can be translated praying. It's used 87 times in the New Testament and describes face to face prayer with God, which underscores intimacy. Praying is more than a mere pop call to the Lord when problems arise or you need something. Praying, in this verse, describes close communion, deep relationship, and intimate companionship with God. I hope that describes your connection with the Lord through the Holy Spirit.

Paul said in verse 18, praying "at all times" which is better stated, praying at the right time. There are two words for time in the New Testament, *kairos* and *chronos*. We live in time that is measurable (*chronos*). That's where we get the word chronology, the calculated arrangement of events. But God is outside our time, so He moves in His time (*kairos*) which is a specific, appointed time by Him.

When we're sourced by the Spirit, we'll find ourselves praying specific, God-ordained prayers that always hit the target. These are prayers prayed at His time, under His leadership. They are specific, direct, and incredibly effective against the enemy. This means the enemy can't outsmart us when we are praying prayers sourced by the Holy Spirit because our prayers dismantle and destroy the works of darkness.

Roman soldiers were trained to throw their lance at the exact moment when their enemy was most vulnerable, thus piercing their heart. Our prayers, when sourced by the Spirit, are not random shots in the dark hoping to hit something, but timely released lances that pierce darkness so heaven can manifest on earth. Yield your heart to the empowerment of the Holy Spirit and ask Him to source both watching and praying in your life.

PRAYER POINTS

- Take a moment to thank the Lord for the presence and power of the Holy Spirit.
- Ask God for a Spirit of discernment. Pray that your spiritual eyes and ears are open.
- Pray for a deeper intimacy and communion with the Lord.
- Ask the Lord to give you specific, timely prayers; targeted prayers led by Him.

CHAPTER SEVEN

UPROOTED SELFISHNESS, UPTURNED GAZE

Corey Jones

Over the past few years, I've mourned and lamented over numerous ministers who have failed and fallen, denominations that have departed from sound doctrine and divided, and schools that once trained missionaries and ministers that have sadly closed.

I've felt the warnings in my heart to never cast stones, because Jesus is coming as a refiner's fire for all of us (Malachi 3:2-3), revealing everything that is hidden, especially hypocrisy (Luke 12:1-3). He's exposing the very thoughts and intentions of every heart (Hebrews 4:12). Scripture warns that a time of shaking is coming that will reveal everything that can be shaken, referring to created things, so that what remains is God's unshakable kingdom (Hebrews 12:27).

As I attempted to intercede and ask the Lord to spare these ministers, ministries, and movements, I experienced strong checks and tender rebukes from the Lord. Yes, Satan is behind all the sinful collapses, but it's God who is ultimately at work. As I prayed for a dear pastor friend who had fallen, I heard the Lord say to me, "Corey, I'm not concerned about titles or legacies, but about the condition of My people's hearts. When I come, My Bride will be pure and made ready."

After reflecting on these words, the Spirit directed me to a passage in the book of Jeremiah which I believe is so instructive and insightful regarding God's ways and purposes in this season:

> "This is what the Lord, the God of Israel, says to you, Baruch: You said, 'Woe to me! The Lord has added sorrow to my pain; I am worn out with groaning and find no rest.' But the Lord has told me to say to you, 'This is what the Lord says: I will overthrow what I have built and uproot what I have planted, throughout the earth. Should you then seek great things for yourself? Do not seek them. For I will bring disaster on all people, declares the Lord, but wherever you go I will let you escape with your life'" (Jeremiah 45:2-5).

Why would God add sorrow to our pain? Why would God allow us to groan, finding no rest? Is it possible that what we're witnessing today by the demise of ministries and movements has been orchestrated by God? That God, not Satan, is bringing down and overthrowing what He built? Could it be the Lord is uprooting things He planted? To be clear, I'm not actually claiming that's what is happening in any specific situation, but I leave open the possibility that what looks like a tragedy could be God's mercy at work.

Why would God do such a thing? This prophetic passage in Jeremiah reveals that whenever we seek our own renown or glory, our own selfish agendas, or when we forget how dependent we are on God, that He won't hesitate to intervene to *rescue* us from ourselves, our pride, and even our success. When we form allegiances and alliances that aren't by His Spirit, it seems God won't hesitate to intervene to overthrow and uproot things He planted (Isaiah 30:1).

The Lord's warning through Jeremiah is reminiscent of Paul's words in Corinthians, "For no one can lay any foundation other than the one already laid, which is Jesus Christ. If anyone builds on this foundation using gold, silver, costly stones, wood, hay or straw, their work will be shown for what it is, because the Day will bring it to light. It will be revealed with fire, and the fire will test the quality of each person's work. If what has been built survives, the builder will receive a reward. If it is burned up, the builder will suffer loss but yet will be saved—even though only as one escaping through the flames" (1 Corinthians 3:11-15).

I believe we're entering a time when God's fire is testing the quality of our works, efforts, and ministries. I pray that what we've built and devoted our lives to can survive God's consuming fire.

The way we can ensure that what we've built survives the coming fire of judgment is by keeping everything, including ourselves, on the altar of personal and corporate prayer. Scripture reminds us the fire on the altar is to never go out (Leviticus 6:12-13). Sadly, we've witnessed throughout history altars that once burned with fire fall into ruin through disuse (1 Kings 18:30). This always leads to *Ichabod*, the departing of God's glory (1 Samuel 4:21-22).

P. F. Bresee, the founder of the Church of the Nazarene, would often challenge Nazarenes to keep an "upturned gaze" which is a call to fervency and faithfulness in prayer. Bresee warned that movements can easily become distracted and fall into worldliness and sin, but if there is one person who will look up and set their gaze upon the Lord in prayer, God promises to pour out the glory of His Spirit and presence again. Listen to Bresee's hopeful warning and call:

> "The depth of our gaze into heaven is the measure of our strength to do God's work. Nothing but the light and fire of the divine presence which comes along this soul-gaze into the heavens can so

fuse the soul that it can burn up the driftwood of worldliness and sin, and pour its streams of power to save out among men. It is strange how organizations tend to get choked with worldliness, and the grace of God ever pushing catches the upturned gaze of men and women and opens through them new channels. We have come to the testing time. If the channels are kept open, God's grace will continue to flow through us to men."

PRAYER POINTS

- Pray the prayer David prayed, asking the Lord to search your heart and try you (see Psalm 139:23-24).
- Ask Jesus if you are forming allegiances or alliances that the Holy Spirit has not prompted. If so, take some time to repent and turn unto the Lord.
- Ask the Lord to root out all selfishness and give you an upturned gaze—setting your eyes on the Lord.

NEXT STEPS

Describe what the Holy Spirit taught you while reading this book?

How can you build a sustaining culture of prayer in your life? What about in your church?

What are your greatest challenges to sustaining a lifestyle of prayer?

Ask the Holy Spirit to direct you to several people who can agree in prayer with you.

What are some specific things you've recently heard from the Lord as you prayed?

What are some take-aways from this book?

ABOUT the AUTHORS

COREY JONES and his wife, Beth Ann, pastor Crossroads Tabernacle (CT) in Fort Worth, Texas. For nearly thirty years, CT has impacted people across the nation and around the world. The story of CT has been heard by thousands; a church that nearly closed and a pastor who nearly quit. Today, CT is a house of prayer that has witnessed impossible miracles, redemption stories, and deliverances through prayer. They are carrying the mantle of praying morning, noon, and night, and CT is raising up generations of prayer warriors including young people who have a heart to seek the manifest presence of God.

For more information, go to:

CTgiveshope.com

pastorcorey@ctgiveshope.com

ROB MCCORKLE and his wife, Cindy, are the founders of Fire School Ministries. After thirty years of pastoring and leading a church that experienced continuous revival, they entered itinerant ministry. While Cindy teaches and mentors from home, Rob travels the nation teaching, training, and equipping pastors and leaders in churches of all sizes and many denominations. Fire School has published many books and resources that equip believers to remain Scripture fed and Spirit led.

For more information, go to:
FireSchoolMinistries.com
fireschoolministries@gmail.com

FIRE SCHOOL PRAYER INTENSIVES are conferences led by Corey Jones and Rob McCorkle focusing on prayer and its connection with the Holy Spirit, revival, spiritual authority, city transformation, and other related topics.

For scheduling, go to:
fireschoolministries@gmail.com

NOTES

NOTES

NOTES

NOTES

NOTES

NOTES

NOTES

NOTES

NOTES

NOTES

NOTES

www.ingramcontent.com/pod-product-compliance
Lightning Source LLC
LaVergne TN
LVHW050943080826
845145LV00004B/1395

* 9 7 8 1 9 5 3 2 8 5 7 2 0 *